the Falling Place

New & Selected Poems About Love

Larry Kuechlin

Alabaster & Mercury
Ocean Beach, California

Kuechlin, Larry
the Falling Place, New and Selected Poems About Love; p. cm
ISBN-13: 978-0615919386 (paper : alk. paper)
ISBN-10: 0615919383 (paper : alk. paper)
Copyright © 2013 by Larry L. Kuechlin, Jr.
First Edition.

All rights reserved. Printed in the United States of America. No part of this book may be used or reproduced in any manner whatsoever without the express written permission except in the case of brief quotations embodied in critical articles and reviews.

Published by:
Alabaster & Mercury
Ocean Beach, California, USA

Many of these poems were previously published in periodicals.

Also from Larry Kuechlin:

Mountain Biking Orange County
Randy Vogel and Larry Kuechlin, Globe Pequot Press

Along a Ruined Sea
d/e/a/d/b/e/a/t/ Publishing

Along a Ruined Sea: Special Edition
Avalon Press (2010)

Entrances: 30 Poems and 100 Lines About Love
Avalon Press (2011)

Something Still Visible In the Fire
Alabaster & Mercury, 2012

elemental
Alabaster & Mercury, 2012

for Alba

Contents:

7: Acrylic On Canvas
8: the Falling Place
10: I Turned
14: Slowly We Love
15: Journey
18: Late Statice
19: Continuing
20: A Fisherman's Hands
22: Botticelli Blues
26: the Cool Side of the Bed
30: Through (After Neruda)
32: Lies In the Rain
33: Laying In a Field Watching the Clouds Roll By
34: Something Still Visible In the Fire
35: Naming Stars
38: The Fifth Stage
44: Our House
45: Window
48: I Dreamed the Sea Was Silent
50: Calculating Heaven
52: days end
53: Tornado Alley
54: Love Song for Nobody
56: Run-off
58: Entrances
62: Faith
64: And Slowly
65: Something We Left Behind

Manifesto

*the danger of irises
is beautifully
pallid;*

they cannot be unseen

*a failure
upon which
to measure your*

striving.

*you read my words
but do you hear me?*

*I would burn every poem
I have ever written
to hold someone's hand
for a single day*

as if they meant it

Acrylic on Canvas

Contained in Waterford crystal,

mangos and pears sliced open;
left to bear the weight of
the beautiful blade that bid them asunder.

       Croissants and blackberry jam;

a forward stroke of sunlight
a staccato return of amethyst and
                    soft laughter;

silver flatware bearing fresh butter
left abandoned, next to a small volume on the table

    Keats, Thomas,   Neruda
          (the sigh is all the same)

dog-eared and worn open
by a missing hand;

dark coffee, dark sugar
and a damp towel draped over an empty chair:

      forward strokes of earth rich red;
      a kiss of black on the return.

The negative spaces fill themselves.

Today,

my heart left my body
and became a light my soul could follow home

but light can be so difficult
when your brush is tangled up in the stars.

The Falling Place

a path that will not lead
though many steps have cut its length

water descends
                gathers
    and tumbles once more

warm stones hold the river on its course
as branches burn a quiet incantation;

a place where memory will not follow
and everything is falling wingtip away:

the valley hesitates
    beneath a mist of heather and sienna

                    the hills
                            drift

drift beneath darkly these lines we forget with a sigh

the poetry of cicadas and release
rising through the tired old Dogwoods;
words unspoken that languish
unhidden between us;

footfall and fingertips
weave their own kind of silence:

in the falling meadow,
just beyond the last shadows,
we watch evening dance the entwined length
of our limbs and song;

you ask me if I can arrange the heavens
into the thinnest of veils

but I am already lost in the sound of
        your skin against a ramble of naked stars:

lay with me in the moon and mourning:
bring to me your whispers;
        satin from the mouth of slow fire:

recite them to me
falling through light and eternities
        in languid motions of soft requital

here in this place
where worlds end and your name begins

I Turned

Imagining laughter
I turned

heartlong into a
beauty of
light clattered
nightfall,
bruised silken
by a deeply
hummingbird brushing…
whorled magnificent
into the eyeful
desires
of seraphim
skies
and ruby soothed
gold.

And I heavenly marveled

imagining
my only nightwardly
transfixed world
indecently sunward and
fire lavished
upon this Shiva-kissed
suddenly
grace;

I turned
from the sharded
meanderings
of my wavered life;

I turned
as everything
wind-torn tiredly will:

ash down and
mindfully echoed into the
emptier sense of my utter
unsleeping.

I have wasted my life
edging the run of horizons
from the farther chance
of openly living:
imagining clarity
across the cluttered page;
dying by degree,
into the rusting
degrees.

For I am the
spilling of words and
endless blood…
I am turning emptiness
enfolding forlorn
into this only sky that has
wiped my eyes golden
into a farther

hoping;

a dream unburdened of the
hopelessness I yet carry
in these languished arms:
to be, once more willing
to hold all the sadness
wept from every
angel burnished heaven:

willing me to carry
the heaviest of all burdens:

hope.

And I am oceans done.

I will never know poetry again:
I will never sing the stars
from their delightedly,
sleep drowned sea;

I will never know the moon
or the rumored pale
it hushes onto
unsuspectfully dawdled,
foot-bare souls:

I cannot
understand these outside
the contexting Lux
of your fragrant, every

being.

I will ever,
only breathe
you.

I will only

(mattering little
to the very littleness
of a heart I hold in
my word-madly song spinning)

ever only hear your sounds
from a dove-turned
softly darkness,
in the facile any knowing I have;
my fractured
fumblings of just this
deafness of a
heart

and dancingly immaculate,

rose rained

yours:

with all the
burning

joyously

our honey mingled hands
can whisperingly away tease
from a sun tuliped vast,
and the nightingales of our
lily starred persistency,
kissed sapphire eternal

between.

Slowly We Love

where we fell

where the snow gathers sunlight to itself

in the moment before the quiet reconciliation
of Dawn and slowly sorrow

our days appear in such a languid grief
along their white way;

      left to find a deceit

or an impression deep enough
to carry winter through its cold slumber

there have been so many steps covered

forward becomes a circle that leads
us back upon our imperfections

a clearing left in briefly the song and stars

hand to hand,
dancing December through and through

      turning just to turn

circles covered in softly a broken sky

an Ash stand bows a gentle yellow hand;
encircles the breath left to light

and light left only
to the steps that remain

Journey

¿Pequeño Hermano, en dónde has vagado?

    I have come home

here, where
the water is full of my anguish,
with the same questions
the sun, in its
        resolute dying
will not answer;
a conversation held across the heart's shadow
and the Sunset Cliff's patient drift
    beneath time and recanting sea.

A young Dusky has followed
the warm currents along Point Loma
to feed in the shallows below me.

    I recognize him by the scars he bears.

He comes back to
remind me of memory and seasons;
old photographs that bleed to vanish
into the turned up corners of
        the tired wish,
and all the worn places
where the sun hides a burnished face.

He reminds me of days
when I followed the unpaved ends of Baja 1
beyond the wildflowers of Vizcaino

into the arms of Santa Rosalia;

French croissants and strong coffee
cutting the cold nectar from chilled mangos

                on a morning terrace
languid over colorful clapboard houses
hewn from the strength of the Copper Armada,
and plazas filled with the reminisce of dance;
past the Cathedral of Eiffel
and the invisible sea of Concepcion

            to La Paz
where he raced along my Whaler
in the lee of Isla Cerralvo
just there, where the song of the Finback
drops away to eternity

into hands that remain empty
even under the impossible weight
of a drowning moon over
                    Bahia de Los Angeles:

memories that
dip a finger into San Borja night
and stir a sky absolved
under the insistent whisper
                    of Milky Way:

        there is so much more to light
        than remembrance...
        there is so much

more...

until finally I understand
I am seeing with
            my heart;
that he is young
only when the sky is young
under a borrowed fire held
            summer long.

I stand along shore
amidst the echo of sea shells forgetting slowly light;

and I wish to follow him
where no journey can equal its steps;
to find the loss of things,
        adrift   as disconsolate;
to swim out to the edge of the La Jolla abyss
beneath following trades
            bruised with gold;
and carry them with me in
               3 great breaths;
deeper than hope;
     deeper than stars;

to leave my breath in the light that remains
on the razors edge of sight;
and look back up in that moment
when the sun has remembered
        breadth and passing
and seeks its place where it has always been;
             without falling or time;

to look up beyond
that final pinpoint of light:

     just then,

your hair descends down from dreaming
and my arms are full of answers

     and I realize
I have ever only had but
               one journey:

     I've spent my life
listening to the wind   plead
wingfuls of reaching fire
        over the confession of sun to sea

and every word was
       your name.

Late Statice

in the poplars
the sun is everywhere
surrounding cold footsteps
                quiet breaths

along the path
October flows into everything;

branches speak of calico and September
and we look for things that hold the morning still

here, a flash of late Statice in early frost;
a drift of fallen stars hiding amongst casual leaves

even rust seems new in the heavy ocean dew

it seems odd to speak of summer now;
the distant lie, Spring
              in the rising autumn sun

you take my hand
and I feel your blood continuing:

we do not pick the season
only the astonishment

Continuing

Upon water and unison,
the fire:

upon genesis
and all these silent matters:

our hands continuing;

the imperfect stars ringing
where scars are hewn;
a reflection of incite and fall
laid to rest over landscapes rising up.

Upon wing light and knowing,
the sky, waiting;
and restless night beyond;

our breath continuing;

the pathways of our bind,
touched as helpless;
uncloaked within a shadow length of

sudden words;
convergence as one darkness

becomes another.

A Fisherman's Hands

The Sea of Cortez
holds no keepsakes
in the bleach and bone.

I walk the hour of wings
when the gloam of you
sings the wind to silk
under this empyrean wheel
of heaven to white;

cast my net upon umber and shine
with hands cut rough to salt;

and you are softer than moonlight.

And in the fleeting,
snow wavers dream jade under an egrets gaze,
as Frigates spire the dark drifts of flame,
and avocets stride the dying
                                    fire.

At the market once, I saw you
across the call of merchants;
and you stood silent against a sky,
buckled under your
                grace, and drifted so.

And I thought,
        just once,

I could touch you;
I could reach into
                your smile

and touch you where the light of you

would not be worn away
under the rough ends of my days, and

your eyes would hold me

just once,

        precious
in those seconds

before life washed back over your sight;

but you were gone.

And in this hour I cast a tired net,
as my hands fall oceans deep
upon the waters of
                Cortez;

still

I see you

through clenched eyes and dreaming; clearly
in the tides that run black and light;

I leave my life strewn towards you
in the sands along a ruined sea
      when just

fire lays upon gold,

and lament the moon
among many birds.

Botticelli Blues

I still see you,
there, in the moment of
lamplight and veils,
when tones of ocean
carry me dream long
back to my falling:

> lust on marble steps;
> without compare in the crush
> of hurried humanity:
> an illumination of
> iniquity and black leather,
> settled as Venus
> into your deliberate eyes;

I see your steps
forever down the Esplanade
morning away, where and always
the fade of you drifts me down
the Botticelli Blues.

I remember you at the Loreto Plaza:

an asphalt artisan;
ancient masters and chalk;
he sang slowly the wind
into his words.
Each drop of silver cast
set our Met dream
deeper at our feet:
the day we stood before
Van Gogh and Botticelli:
Starry Night and
The Birth of Venus;
your name by any other flower:
a siren of Pagan flame;

a contrition of faith
that drew me towards the
            winnower's light.

Inside the Insomniac Café,
across a beatnik sea of
berets and manifestos;
a barista allegro
of strong coffee in chipped cups;
we read each other
allusions and Beat Poet slang
Nina sang our torch red conclusions
under tattered pictures of
Kerouac and Waits.

At the incendiary ends of
vanilla and conjure;
lost in your stray:
I stole your kiss to Myles;

and in a rift the Bird set aloft,
you stole it right back.

We spoke back beat lies;
the heart dawned heresies
of star wild skies;
an evening sigh upon
closely shoulders:

against my hunger,
you deepened your smile
double 4 time
and danced away.

And I remember you there

at Sangria,
in close currents of desire;
the raven of you drew me out
into the Birth of Coltrane Cool:

bailaron; bailaron...

a touch and retreat of
gazes and fingertips;
pirouettes of laughter and grazes
falling careless from hungry lips,

and you; just;
your vagaries and spell
that stained my vision and hope
across a stolen beat
that sounds for only you;

soothed away,
sinuous in your rhythms and skirt,
under a meandered smile:

> *flamenco puede solamente ser fuego*
> *fuego puede solamente ser danza*

and when your sway settled to my hands;
when I held your arch and soar
I whispered:

> *solamente cielo*
> *solamente viento*
> *solamente asimiento*

your eyes, a dark burnish of secrets and flight:

> *solamente hermosa; solamente usted*

Just there,
in serenades and relinquish,
you turned:

> breath lips fire death

and I remember,

the way drowning holds the sea,
our endless fall
into Silver Strand;
Veuve Clicquot bled out;
a sacrifice to our reckless burn
there, in the pagan hours of
Botticelli blue;

remember
your bodice laced only in moon;
just you; hewn of starlight in
forgotten shades of beautiful;
your skin; a honeyed taste of
sunset and sin;

remember our bodies,
deeper than turning and surrender
curving as encircled night, hungry as lost;
speaking words heard only in iris.

You set your mouth to flame
towards heavens you never knew;
dipped your hair into a kiss of
dawn and Milky Way,
burning as sunder;
a linger, shadow spent to
abandon and gold,
while morning watched
the unison of Venus
writhe deep in jade hands.

The Cool Side of the Bed

                You were always cold
sleeping under the open window;
but it was yours, alone.

Through months when I could barely breathe,
the Pacific's soothing regress through
the misshapen arms of that old Torrey Pine
                        always set you to chill;

even in the disquiet of my night's passing,
you covered yourself and would not relent,
        as I continued to burn.

Living by the sea,
       you learn about wind;
how it is not driven across deserts and distances;
it's drawn into the cold vacancy left as heat rises:
the disparate need of physical forces
to find their equilibrium.

These are the sleepless truths I hold on to.

The blinds waver through a wind laced with Milky Way,
          empty arms in a forgotten motion of sleep,
and I wonder where my dreams have fallen
among these subtle sounds that keep my eyes reaching
all through the creaseless night.

There will be no dreams: there never are;

just this fleeting balance of darkness and memory.

And there is a moment
just a shimmering moment in the shiver before tomorrow

before the shuffle of slippers across oak floors
before the bedroom lights and coffee cups
before the car doors and embraces

when in the lightless silence I hear love
so casually left on the mist and concrete;

those little,
        fleeting motions of love
that sear my heart to such essential starlight

                and I wonder if,
in the weightlessness of all I have since wanted
I could once more turn to you in the soft aftermath
half lit in ways only abandon can bring

and whisper you across the line where
                         slowly fire deigns:
careless riddles of scarlet undoing
falling tip to tip in the undark torrent.

And I would tell you
I still remember the way your breasts move
under satin and Poseidon's pale touch;

        remember everything scattered along love's rescission;

the deft cries left in the months without food,
when I denied myself to stand by you,
                and became everything and nothing;

when I learned even hunger has a purity
as I staggered down the stairs behind you
until I could hear the sound of my own words
outstretched into red lights and rain;

      screams that fell no farther than my hope

and there,
among the lies and lacerations that bleed
beneath every knee yielded to wet pavement
          I would show you that silence has a purity as well;

and long after, when there are no more words;
when emptiness crafts our final embattlements

even then,
      I would take your hand

and lift you up into this new remembrance of
what we thought we both knew;

      over and softly, our hands;
lost as sky in the impression of ascension
all through this fall of silk and absolutes

to once more,
      burdened as light
find the touch stones of our elemental truths
in the blind hours of our wonderment

wings wheeling and air comingled in a closer heat;
eyes dance the emerald miles;
      water and the white repose;

earth and a reign of fire rising,

                burning it all away
until, in the final motion, our hands can hold
the souls weight in the stratum of denial.

    I often think of your new husband and child

passing the prayer torn hours,
one arm left stillborn on the cool side of the bed
blinds, desperate to find the beat of life in an indifferent wind;

heaven casts a silver clatter down
                upon rooftops and swayback sills;
and all through this rain, the hymn of cold candles,
        flush to the creases of our sorrow;

the equilibrium of contrition and a closing window

an open hand reflects a moonless sky

light without mercy; time without void

                untethered and unknown;

    the dire mass of a dying sun.

Through
(After Neruda)

in this place

    this wind

this fragment of darkness
left unimpeded against a burning world

    I loved you as water through water

here, where oceans,
    breath by moon,
tear the world away from its
    ephemeral solidarity:

the waves forming each other
in a collision of momentary beauty
and sound we once held as solitary truth:

sand   shells   smooth stone;

words rushing through water
just as quickly carried to darkness;

an eternal rescission of firmament
    to such profound rest:

tides that seek redemption for all
the soft imperfections that make them whole.

and in memory we can only hold at night
I have waited here
    for you

as life through life
    the heavens turn away:

a seabird,
turning its head under wings that will not fly,
burning white against slowly the last silhouette;
hiding in the beautiful shadow of its plaintive cries:

      hearts and daylights dim

a glow that recedes across my open palms
bringing the cold distances of space in depth

as light through light
      the stars die in my arms

and I seek redemption for being my only scar
in darknesses yet unknown.

Lies In the Rain

Outside the Hurricane Café;

The night in its tantrums
          goes about its noisy descent;
silver into rising smoke,
a coy drift that shuffles its long way to dark.

I recite you Eliot
          in the hush of huddle;
couplets upon the desire where your dreaming starts.

When,
finally the old words of Seattle
whisper upon us night in brittle silences,
              frail as October flowers;
I can see star broken blue,
fathomless and impatient for the pen.

Why won't Seattle rain on me?

You settle further into my warm
as I breathe you in,
          vanilla and laughter;
and your eyes are a sapphire shade of scarlet
and your hair is tangled in my sighs as I turn,

and you grab my jacket collar and draw me back;

      I wish this rain would stop…

I can feel drops of it on my shining as
Seattle sings to us stillness and dance,
in this compromise of heat, leaning against the night.

I hold your smile,
          burning upon moon stained hands,

as we complete the softly lie.

Laying In a Field Watching the Clouds Roll By

the daisies are yellow
not that it matters, but today
        it is universal truth

I can feel their color here and there
              beneath your hand

hours stretch into seconds

and the dream surmises
        I don't believe in a first kiss;
the kiss that all others are measured by

I wonder why there is such sadness in the world
when your eyes tell me every kiss is our first
              and every breath; our last

we find shapes in each embrace; wayward sun

the ocean winds are overwhelmed
in wildflower and slow laughter

seconds stretch into starfall

I allude to your shoulders; curves;
the soft narrative in my hands

you allude to your clothing

the daisies are red
      not that it matters

but tonight, I feel them burning
beneath your hands

Something Still Visible In the Fire

These simple moments

      a ring filled with black oak

the moon meanders sapphire definitions
as heaven whispers through mesquite

smoke
curling or encircling
    and closer now in fire's flight;
imperfections released
           in the flow to ash

fingertips find the beautiful distance
as we trace wings into the sky

    the wind draws a bow across the stars
        and the imperceptible movement
behind hands we extend to find heat

these simple moments.

Naming Stars

Why do we name
                stars?

    Aries Capricorn Orion

Mere words;

such arrogant folly
under the Pan
          theo
n of never ending and
light.

Perhaps, their names
             without syllable or context
should be only sound;
something worn sun smooth to

insinuation;

a sonata redolent of chestnut
falling to
            endless recur,
or
      an etude of moonsift
through mingled arms.

Listen with me just now

here
against the brand
        of clover beneath your

            sigh

for a time and distance

when, somnolent as   lost,
your resting
is languid where just
my life

remains;

I'll trace from darkness to void
these spaces where gods
cannot soar

     'till I find just one
near that place where perfect
collides with

                redemption

; lingered along the curve of earth beneath
our necessity

and we(radiance,
         unyielding requiem
)give them sound:

an echo down the promiscuity of
an angel's lattice;

humbled before
ancient pillars of night
broken under the Elysium of
         just one.
And when,
     fire to light,

our hands
entwine heaven's last hour
and we
     settle
under the blur of breathless becoming

eternity;

with this simpleton's heart

I see,

in lasting where only
               my eyes can stay;
a solitary faith
imbued in concupiscent star,
    a billion light years
beyond coalesce or the rain
of fallen gods;

and here, amidst the
simple weave of only and

only

I cannot remember
why I am crying

       but none of this matters:

there is
no heaven deeper
than

you.

The Fifth Stage

And now even when I can no longer see
I continue to arrive at words
                      The Blind Seer of Ambon, W.S. Merwin

Baja breathes
            a dissonance of desires:
elemental seams of slow passage
across the withered strata of
no arrival
        and no way back.

Wingtips swallow the darkness
of Boojum and desert palms;
            find the sky-born edge of sapphire
as sun-choked stones
                that once held a blind sea
cobble an indifferent star
to burn life into wavered focus.

You hold a curled shade
                    deep into your sleep:

        an errant lock dreams of flight;
        sundresses and the black sway of falling satin.

On parts drawn out of
              the silt of Laguna Chapala,
the old Blazer jostles down
the crossroads of home:
              a sentient detour away from La Paz.

I watch you amidst the
weathered sound of heavy tread along Baja 1

reminding us both;
                      home.

Up the grade at El Rosario,
past the burnt out reminder of a passenger bus:

windows full of foxtail and ash;
        melted rubber and heavy rust;
crosses lean a worn shoulder
                      into road dust and fire-splayed diesel;
     plastic flowers and grave faces:
a lover's faded pilgrimage;
            an angel's each descending wish;

I watch
    a solitary pangero
make his way across
        the peal of Bahia San Quentin
under staves of the burning harvest.

The Mariner 45 strains under his haul;
        red urchins for the bustle of Japanese markets.
Under the watchful eye of Isla Guadalupe
he risks his life for a breeze full of yen.

Bonita Sharks and bad air
              thin his brother's blood;
a scarlet horizon
that sets a crinoline stain
              on the Blessed Mother.

His bowline turns
        falling and forever,
    a groove worn gold-deep in time
as he shores his boat under
the stream-fall of a solitary Coleman,

there, against the aged grey of a tide weary shack.

And as daylight deifies a fleeting streak of doubloon
and arms gather an open bind of return,
I wonder what quietly heaven carries
                into the only space beyond relent:

        a shawl curling into night stained tile;
        a thigh brushed into flame-pulsed heaven.

And I wonder

as shutters are closed to
        everything but flight
and she listens to his heart
                whisper promises and mescal:

is it those moments that
set our fierce steps homeward
against our own mortality and echo:
                can we yet hear loves faint siren
in the dark moments of deal
when our cries fall prayer deep into the wind,
and hope is spent

crafting wings from an armful of rain?

At the only stop sign in Hidalgo
                      I turn off Baja 1
up the valley towards
the Mission de San Telmo;
        push carts hobble a musical strain
shoulder down in wind-creased promise:
the iron pot clatter of sun-dust disarray
                glass jars cast a verdant gleam
                olives and cold pressed oil
                a staccato dance of fire-roasted peppers
                laced into fresh-picked jalapenos.

Mercado Isabel bustles under
the failing daylight of a Pacific cloak
       a bag of roasted Pistachio's
              pesos fall loosely into the rhythm of her days.

A white shawl covers her face
but not her eyes,
             no:
    she is the strength of Sierra Gigante
    she is the grace that gambols every facet of Cortez dawn.

In a star brambled crook
        above the long meadow
the Blazer rambles a dandelion legato.

Years meander a fence line
       that fades away to forgotten,
here amidst the cobalt winds of San Pedro Matir.

We spread the rough wool
       of Mexico beneath us
as sycamores settle their restless hands
into a tangle of summer in Milk Thistle
              and early moon.

A young colt has joined us from the shadows;
rust ideas of brown and black
        standing over white socks.
He places a nose over tired barb wire
to eat the sliced apples you hold;
             rubies in your open hand.

I watch juice run wrist-down your delight.

He has lost his will to
      restrain,
    content in your palm;

I borrow slowly the other
              (this is how I see.)

The colt glides sotto voce into his joy
and we watch time slip the calico draft
                cottonwood deep to dissipate.

 We eat dates purchased under the
                serpentine shadows of Rio Mulege;
fresh cotija and pineapple empanadas
from the little bakery beneath
                the palms of Catavina;

San Vincente Cabernet filled to
                the Waterford edge;

oaks trees brush tired notions
into the blur of you and I
                scherzando dolce

      a winding and refrain

      the red of Baja earth in a woven fist
shoulder to   sigh
                wings

dark truffles and prayer offered on
                a waiting breast:

    draw down
        down the starry deign;
    paint our silences in faint words of
        fingertips and claire de lune;

weary colors hue the lilting drift
                Mourning Dove and dew

hands find their way   always further;

      hush

a koan of

    crescendo and never more

        listen

the last words of ocean
      speak indiscreet fire

    and I come to know
as hearts cross
        the whisper's length
to find a higher source of the sun:

      I am
          no longer.

Our House

it wasn't the way your eyes
danced across accidental words
of thinly veiled starlight

or the silence
      captured in the collision
of a hand so very far away against your breast

it was the smile you gifted me
as you lowered slowly your head
and listened to my heart catch up to

                                  forever

Window

I could hardly glance at you...

The sky has forgotten to fall

upon my eyes,
fall in this light after
                light;

which, against heaven

Junipers murmur
obsidian to white:
Pinon sleep a quiet lilt,
as quail tuck their dreams
              whiskey away;
and into the collapse of peacefully
vermillion:

lies now calico into evening;
lies now diamond to wing

among the hands that spill their blue
upon this covenant of candle
              and canyon sway.

Breathes the night;

you have forgotten me...

A voice I can no longer hear

in this place where I have stood
and never walked;

ancient words,
windborne to cedar
I have stood with
heart to heart in their ages;

epochs of soul,

worn sand smooth in long whispers
that spill through mesquite
across the dark hearth of desert time
and mesas patient in white drift.

And into the rising,
still in the ancient tongue;
I set you

Morning Star

deep upon the darkly glass;

a flare;

you move through me,
dressed only in sky;
a reflection in frost;

an intimacy of breath
we have forgotten to hear;

and in this place where
you have walked, but never

stood;

an open hand tangles a stray caress;
        moon to the touch;

an illumination;

phantom close among lazily arms;

and now

lies the quail, startled as sun;
lies the chestnut and curve;
lies the softly and burn

of light upon
eyes not forgotten
to

stars.

I Dreamed the Sea Was Silent

Under a sky torn from half dark sails
for you,
    I dreamed the sea was silent
all across the rage white shoals,
as the wind rolled Poseidon's cold farewell
into December gales.

And weaving the sounder's sad tale,
round White's Point and Portuguese Bend
the wheelhouse keeps watch as I turn down my coat
and shiver a few more miles under Orion's grist
while sirens turn their long light over locks and quay.

And when at last through Angel's Gate,
morning pulled from darkness and moored tight,
I walk the slow sounds of gunnels rock and rise;
a low, homeward yawn across the dock's pale ring
as the boys sing a Bell's half goodbye.

And through a sea mist that
prays the grey cobblestones back to you,
I follow my turned down boots through alleyways
where the clapboard candles burn alone
    in the heel of the dark;

up to softly the solemn door,
these months left just a satin stir from opened;
and turn the bright kept brass
polished a thousand times in her hearts hand;

and as my night coat falls
moonlong into the porch's quiet refrain
and a forgotten wick burns near bare feet;

I hold you in hands worn beyond worth;

and lift you higher than wings hewn white with eternal array
until you find all the stars that speak your name:

and beneath heaven's shame, bow my head
                    the distance that deepens even light,

eyes wavering on the silent edge of lost
as they whisper you words an old fisherman's unworthy to speak

and every one of them means beautiful.

Calculating Heaven With an Ashton Cigar and Taylor Fladgate Port

It has been said
that the odds of DNA,
        purely by chance
becoming what we know it to be
calculates out to
        10 to the 260th power;

roughly equal to the number of
        every single particle here on earth;

each with their own calculations
and rough pathway of
        fragile mutations;
still,
    just one single step along
the eternal baseline of everything we are.

I add a little Taylor port to the Ashton VSG
as I stand at the Porch and watch
a conversation between fire
        and constellations becoming
curl away into a long sigh.

People who track such things will tell you
it took 2 million people, from field to market
to provide me this moment
    drenched in sun-forged perfection;

from the hands stained deep of
Nicaraguan soil and cultivation's embrace
to the hand that wears a familiar groove into the binnacle
as it guides the freighter into port.

I love to stand near the ocean at night

a darkness with limits,
                    yet lost
to perceive motion by faith or need;
to look for stars so far away,
                    or so it is said
their light,
     without ending,
will spill across the entire span of earth's history
and still never find its place in our heaven.

I lift my right arm
just as you glide up in silence behind me
to lock your arms around my waist;

          look up to the Source of light

as you rest your smile
into a place, forever only yours

and wonder who comes up with these silly calculations.

days end

days end

and the road deepens,
        winding down a wind full of calico doubt

late October lays its head
heavy in Poplar thickets and empty bird nests

I remember you
the way autumn stones hold
            sun drifts and heather

the fading stain of a somnolent impression

we are always looking for the dark
as evening fades a slow shade of heaven

            lace windows flicker a lamps reply

across the meadow,
split wood rails moan grey against time
        as a roan whisper
finds the slow silence of early snow

somewhere close
            words, quiet as fire
find their way home in the half light and amber

and all through this restless song

sudden hands
            softly complete

Tornado Alley

All the horses were heavy under the spurs
but that 454 still couldn't drown out
the flood of .38 Special pouring out
of the single in-dash speaker.

Her feet danced out the Suburban window as
she howled into all the wind a buck twenty five could fetch;

sun dress somewhere in the vicinity of indiscreet

curves in all the hungry places
and eyes that took you all the way down.

One of her hands tugged a black, spaghetti strap
with calculated inaccuracy ever closer to heaven
while the other laid restlessly
between the desire for a few more horses
and the need for a 4-wheel lock up
and 15 minutes off the road.

She smiled as the lights in the mirror forced the decision.

I looked down at the double 12
with the fresh scratches from cutting it down;
spent shells rolling around on the mats.

The State Police were shouting my name
when her hand found another realm.

Yeah;

      hells yeah

she was worth it.

Love Song For Nobody

A kiss is just that,
which upon unknowing Spring,
all burning green
entwines wildflowered
into delightful
madness; and
the laughing emerald
of your persistent glances,
alights cartwheeled marvelous
upon any impetuous petal
drifting soulward
before our honey scattered
hearts.

A moon is just that,
which upon a
drunken shore
bows its white mischief
onto our sea pale feet,
and temptfully throws
pearls and naked rubies
upon the muses
dancing gold towards
our always touching eyes:
which upon the
wandering off,
all ocean vagaries
lingers us softly
into a sapphire delicious
undarkness.

A

you and I

is just that

which upon any sky
learned its
songbird suddenly
magic
and every whirl-tilt
heaven
fell seraphim away
to the flame of all
persistent gods,
doomed in their
eternal self frailty:

and,

upon which

I only breathe,
and I,

only beating
to no solitary purpose,

drown indigo still into
whisper-star always

you.

Run-off

I look at the outline of my footprint
there beneath your boot
                      and smile

the sky lays a gentle fire over us;
the shadows are reticent to leave your embrace.

eyes closed into the heavens,
you smile;

      there are skies
the heart cannot hold.

sitting under scars of
ancient Cypress in early spring array

we wait for words

but the Sierras have their own voice;
their own time:

the wind rushing away from snow melt;
the run off of winter towards wildflowers
and oceans dancing sunlit in opal distances.

winter puts a hush on the valley one last time
as you lean into my shoulder.

if God offers an open hand
it comes lined in Dogwood blossoms,
pink in their evening prayers

you look at me;
just a mountain wren alighting a branch
and quickly, quickly a blur of color away

and I realize there are parts of you that
forever should be touching me:

if God could create something
with more stars than beautiful

He would use your eyes.

Entrances

having only one direction
                heaven

and the recalcitrant parry of Pacific
are fractured against the threshold flow of you;

      a canto written in black silk and angels.

I try to close my eyes
      but that is a convenience long since past;
mumble supplications of belief
as I look across a terrace awash
        in the aftermath of your grace.

      I watch you move hush to hush,

there in the darkness
      chased away with all the reticent light
still willing to be held against
a beauty hewn of sun dust and distances.

I move closer to you
hidden by a heart busy counting the regrets
torn from each tatter of courage;

listen to your life's stories
laced in staccato rhythms of veritas and Vox,

and in the reflection of men I will never be;
a reprisal of truth and cheap chardonnay:
      I am the shadow that dies under your closing eyes.

               I falter to the rail
and into the wind I lift hands that will

          every only be filled with winglight;
            whisper the word broken
until the path it has worn into my soul
is wide enough to carry
      your most fleeting touch;

and in that moment
I hear the Ashgar in the ink
      burn from the dark maelstrom:

a life without stories is no life at all.

And if,
      in the entrances,
we could retrace the steps
and forget this constant need
        to claw a heart back to the bleed;

forget every door closed harder than
      rain against a faceless moon,
forget the glances,
        the simple anguish of simple lies
and all the sounds you couldn't possibly have heard:

feigned joy, crafted a laugh too hard
and their love making
        drifting down a world ajar
from a room just a cry too soon from madness;

and deep in the crimson pour,
      through the hour of promises and clenched hands,
          we would know:

a scar without lies, is no scar at all.

And you turn
a response, with perhaps a smile,
        perhaps a scarlet linger;

and I try to form words

torn there in that moment where
acquiesce falls just a blood drop beyond desire
and I long
        silent as falling
to stand with you;
            divide the oceans in a common sigh
and rend gold from a dusting of summer
                  adrift over a liquid memory of November prairies

        but I have never been to the wheat fields

the great expanse that utters
                the very light of America;

my days have passed in depths
that cover me quietly in a finality of blue

                far too deep for breath.

    I dreamed of Swansea again

walked a wound farther than words;
        pearls cast upon the gilded lee of Bristol

and down the hill to Cwmdonkin Park, I came;
beyond the line where light is broken
                into dreaming and the shadow's reply;
watched the brass dalliance of Devonshire coast
        lay a tumbled goldscape into eternal hands

a dream so real
        it almost ceased being an excuse;
almost formed a burning grief beyond fear and gathered loss;
        a blade of truth that fills the blind chamber:

            light will always find an entrance into the broken,
            though not nearly enough to relinquish the dark.

And I write of love, but every word has been a lie:
I have never known love,
                only how I wish it for you to be:

arms weave a world that can be complete
only in the context of a heart
                whose next beat
                              is mine:

the dance of truth in eyes on the jagged edge of starfall:

      a clarity of returning
              forever as fire returning
and lips that brush a sigh too close to abandon

                moonlight broken by your breath

      fingers fold into mahogany

          a button without memory;
                    the satin echo;

softly the hands etched always into your curve:

                this is how I breathe.

Faith

along the shoreline

along the pathways to and from fire
we are held in slowly a motion of memory:

the way the sun remembers our faces;
the way the wind remembers how
        you curl your torso around my arm

sea birds are burnished against sapphire palettes

unseen,
thermals change their paths
along an unexpected dance

inspiration is a matter of movement:
the subtle let of heaven onto currents yet unwritten

we close our eyes and
touch the last sunlight in a deeper way

it is not the idea of flight that draws us to their wings;
    it is the absolute faith in their joy,
things we feel without intuition or circumstance

my hand moves deeper into yours
   as certain early stars soar through eternal riffs

even these pirouettes become a revelation

white hands of water entreat us
but we are only here to breathe abandon
as Terns cry us softly their white jazz:

without proximity,
        these are our moments;
a lessening of weight that imbues our belief

there is always one more way to say

        I love you

And Slowly

Upon and deeply, my eyes; where I see
sinuous against the arch of your truth;
silently your lips in words that cannot be
spoken; in torrents of what can be true

only in the light of our fuse and touch.
And slowly scarlet my breath upon your
supplication; a name you writhe and hush,
low upon the lay of our sun dark pour.

And slowly my soul into your drown; and
in that moment where flame burns lowly
against our hearts; and slowly my hands
upon the smooth of your fire; and slowly

your breasts against my rhythm as I weave
my fingers to dark; and slowly. Slowly.

Something We Left Behind

You were disappointed that I didn't hear voices,

the day we walked in armfuls of close rain
there on the grounds of Westminster Church
amongst the headstones
and the wandering of sycamores
                      into a shadow full of ravens.

   In my heart, it is still there:

 something I left next to
             3 roses that seem forever fading
and a bottle of cognac that's always
                     just a drop away from empty;

but in my hand,
     there was only yours
the day we left behind the
                catacombs and ghosts
to spend some miles
         top down, in a wind full of sighs
and the change of perspective
brought by every hill along the way:

               Nick Drake weaves us down highway 140;

corn stalks,
        October tired and waiting among starlings;
           rows fall under the umber andante;

sounds of the highway cease as
heaven finds an entrance
           through an old Guild and
                  miles of Neruda.

          Southern Pennsylvania now:
gold wanders a bridge closer to night;
another button becomes
     nothing more than memory.

We wind up the next hill:
          Taneytown Road

winter wheat still rising

            boots abandoned to tired oak

     light
and a hand drawing slowly back

storm shutters slightly askew
and lace curtains
          that speak of long hours of snow
in words that can be heard only
beneath quilts
     and the sound of constant hearts.

        Gettysburg,

     and I stand with you on Little Round Top
in the rustle of gold drifting past night;
there, on ground that cannot
         ever be completely quiet again
even in this dusting of autumn silence.

         I look down Chamberlin's hill

               and I am crying

where he stood for an idea; a thread of belief;
     for something he cherished more than life:

to suffer the wound and end the strife;
to let enough blood that it will never fall again:

something you plead in a voice you can never stop hearing.

And there, in a stand of Ash
my heart looks back up the long hill to
        Westminster Church
and a coin left on marble stained a telltale rose;

remembers each step we walked down St. John's:

       slowly the Susquehanna,
                  impatient among the brittle stars
and I can only breathe against the waters burning edge.

     Words that always were, and are.

Afternoon moves a slow shade
              of the moon forgetting;

   the tide whispers something winged and infinite

as slumber streaks a Chesapeake sky;

     time,
        careless as satin, and Havre de Grace
falling down to a single pinpoint
there on an upturned eyelash;
        tremulous or half determined

              hands closing

silence around us
       or through us

    lips cross a threshold that still exhales light

   and something I left
in eyes that seem forever fading
            into sun flurries and sonnets:

  I can't think of another voice I was supposed to hear.

www.ingramcontent.com/pod-product-compliance
Lightning Source LLC
Chambersburg PA
CBHW060427050426
42449CB00009B/2171